Reading Lesson in the Lifers' Wing

*Good wishes
from
F. J. Williams

Spring 2009*

Reading Lesson in the Lifers' Wing

F.J. Williams

PETERLOO POETS

First published in 2009
by Peterloo Poets
The Old Chapel, Sand Lane, Calstock,
Cornwall PL18 9QX, U.K.

© 2009 by F.J.Williams

**A catalogue record for this book is available
from the British Library**

ISBN 978-1-904324-55-3

Printed in Great Britain
By 4word Ltd, Unit15, Baker's Park, Bristol BS13 7TT

ACKNOWLEDGEMENTS

The poems have appeared in *Agenda, Iron, Poetry Review, Planet, New Welsh Review, The Anglo-Welsh Review* and *Poetry Wales*. 'Poem from the Cricket Pavilion' was a prize-winner in the Bridport Poetry Competition. 'The Slave Graves at Butcher's Apron', 'Reading Lesson in the Lifers' Wing' and 'Sweat Club' were prize-winners in the Kent and Sussex Poetry competition. 'Big Daniel's Allotments' was first broadcast on HTV Wales.

Supported by
The National Lottery®
through Arts Council England

to Valerie and Jonathan

CONTENTS

Reading Lesson in the Lifers' Wing

In calico, the lifer's freedom dress
A man arrives to pick his boom-box up.
He smarms his hair and stops each time his face
Reflects in windows, glass and trolley's rack

Of pans, and sees us in our reading group
Becalmed at tables from the dining-room.
He tunes the fight, smoothes in his barrier-cream
Then jabs a left and shadows through the door.

We shuffle through the things we've brought to read:
A racing pink, a fashion page, a pile
Of letters from a life outside, a cracked
And broken Bible stuck on Exodus.

The man who owns it wipes his lips, tunes out
His smoker's cough and reads: "The waters were
Made sweet and they did drink..." till short of air
He halts. A man who's whiskerless and cowed

Pulls out a bill his wife has sent
And speaks from crumpled folds
An old address with fake Italian logo at the top.
As racks of food-trays flatten under shrouds,

Our southpaw, with his radio coming loud
Then dim, transforms us to the boxing-ring,
The ropes, the food, the fire at Pentecost,
How soup boils from the bottom like a crowd.

Big Daniel's Allotments

(Chwilog)

Now when I see well-worked allotments
I remember Big Daniel who kept rain
In barrels and strode about through
Compost smoke. Big in his boots
He chased us from his plot
Like he was scaring rooks off.
And through the window of his lean-to
Was a factory of summer;
Cobwebbed spades and sacks of killer
Waiting for the sun to blow through the sky
And wake the dogs.

I'm passing one summer father for a boy,
Not Daniel or his dogs
But a pickaxe leaning by the shed.
To go and touch and smell the scented
Secrets of allotments, and what it is
To use men's tools ten years too young.

Meanwhile, a tenant, shoulders
Slumping low, brings down a heavy barrow load
Of rubble for a path.

There's a chill as rooks return from winter.

While under this path and crushed like a seedcase
Is the framework thirty summers leave.

Car Dealer

A stapled price-list flutters from his hand
Whose welcome forfeits family, sleep and health
To make the sale. With doors unlocked, his cars
Display their contents to the street, their past

Wiped out with a car shampoo and the team
Of boys whose galvanised buckets have turned
Their work to froth. The dealer demonstrates
Plastic seats, the engine clocked and silent,

Oil cans, cash and business cards, receipts.
The sales girl in the window counts the cash;
And makes, in well-filled jeans, her hair pushed back
A breath that lasts till dawn upon the glass.

Two Minute Photo Booth

Tough on Existentialism
Tough on the causes of Existentialism,
The city centre's photo booth
Wipes out Sartre at a stroke: the time

That never comes again has come again
With DANCE, BANK, EAT across the sky.
In 'must be going can't stay style'
Jazz, joyrides, the attire of Egyptian queens

Where someone's day-trip comes back black
With the weight of night come down
To judge the OK Shoe Shop and photos of the dead
Stored upstairs out of sight, like the man

In rollers, the silent phone, the car and folk
Who'll never move but give
The gathered gaze of night where no-one speaks
The tricky win with little time to live.

Sweat Club

Too weird to fake, in outsize swim wear,
Open toes and charms, the head of personnel
Steps out at 95 degrees, a blur of cloud,
His face wiped out by striplights

And gift of song among the monsoon,
Fog and sunburn of the sauna lounge.
The part-time boy whose demi-tasse of foam
Arrives in drips, demands a smile, a bell-

Shaped curve of growth, and works the soap
Around his lips like shaving in the Med:
His feet sprawled out, the weather lapsed at wet,
In a slop-shirt shouting salary

He lifts his hands to find his throat and sing
The physio's rolling programme in the fitness suite.
A beach made out of sacks and settled
Cloth declares the cult of cleaner roles.

He comes outside, drips water from the swim,
And deals with hair and eyebrows in the glass;
His eyes a single crease,
He hums a line for beauty in the steam.

The Fire Act

We see his haircut first, cropped bald, and know
He's been evicted for his circus act.
His corporation flat scorched black and walls
Destroyed; his visits to the hospital

With burns, and when he caught his breathing back
The council's final notice came to quit.
He follows animals, the high-wire act
And squats before his art as if in thanks

For burning out his home and neighbour's car.
He's hoarse from paraffin and circus crowds,
From acts of turpentine and pokers which
Rejuvenate the homeless, bald and dumb

Like irony, each breath a brand new face
Singing to be fed. Mr. Dynamite,
The shape of doubt before the slapstick clowns,
His flame that turns us green then wipes us out.

The Jesuit Map of the Moon

Refusing its final outline, this sketch
Of sky like ice beneath the sun that flares
To illustrate which of compass, book or gun
Most changed the world; the glare

That lit the east and earth's adjusting
Shores, the smoky fires that burned
Against the dark. With heaven to choose
Why take delight in this; a moon

In pencil hanging in the night,
A cloistered virtue praised,
As the sun comes down for shadow
And the city blurs in flame?

The Great Wall of China

The man in U.S jockey shorts
And wife's unwearied sullenness for shops,
Her tan, the photographs of everywhere we stop,
Mistakes the state potato farm

And thinks it is the Wall. He shuffles
With their squash-bag up the bus.
The tourist guide, the Hasselblad
And wife whose hair is sunburst

Sit behind. In blue exhaust
A bald cart-driver waves. His dark-
Haired wife in the uncut grass stands up
To watch our journey through their field.

Our man in shorts makes nothing of the place,
The tuneless midday concert or the guide.
He steps out in his sweatshirt
Of the San Francisco Bears, surprised

How U.S. astronauts could see the Wall from space.

Poem from the Cricket Pavilion

'The Elvis Presley Look-Alike December Dance'
In motel typeface, 'Admit Two';
The cricket club's all-ticket disco jams
On 'Wooden Heart'. The doorman's

Sneer and specs have made him blind.
In early '60s suit he gestures to the night
To come inside as if we've finished with the day,
Like history done with chest-expander suits

And baggy trouser-legs, and wearing rubber
Presley masks that look like pain succeeds.
Everyone is king; the flesh that comes together,
The dead who rise by the bar and ask for drinks

Where the longest-selling single since the Crash
Leaves out their resurrection, like the prize –
An Elvis Presley photograph that glows –
The love that glows more brilliant as it dies.

Abraham Lincoln at Platt Fields Park

Without Columbus or the car park's April
For the football field, you might be staring
At the Institute of Man-Made Fibres
And listening to the traffic at your knee.
With your inspector's outfit easy to put on
And frown as if you're puzzling out the Bible
As you walk across to the railway-yard;
Birds tampering in the open sky and water

Trembling upward into light. Two steps
And your unteasled shirt of brass is open
At the neck, the city moving legions
Past your feet like colour on a map
Of battlefields. You point across the park
And seem to see 'America Drinks
From Orchards in the Spring' in broken neon read
Where words burn back to blackness by the breeze.

The Slave Graves at Butcher's Apron

Deemed a place of worship by the Temperance League,
The Band of Hope and ten types of church
In Butcher's Apron, you share a page
In the tourist guide with Municipal Awareness year.

Your names, forbidden among the nettle roots
And tulip bulbs, love would have used,
Like words for the blessing of water,
The smell of vanished corn. Born twice

And nameless in the blinding light of love,
The Primitive rhymes cast out their
Ancient prohibition in the root.
Our tourist map repeats your closing times

And clerk of works. The town that
Owns your gravestones in the park
Omits the fire of nettles round the grave
Where blackbirds fly astray into the dark.

16th hole

As if the wrong people had arisen
This team of Funk and Wagnall business men
Gathers on the green plied with blended gin.
They shield the sun away and raise their eyes;
A Free Church meeting praying for the bar.
Someone marks a score sheet; who's risen,
Who's to rise at their harumphing general
Verdict of the day. From weeks of working
Late, of big demand, the market's slightest
Gesture of fatigue, our team comes loudly
Forth like Extreme Brethren at the daub of
Rouge. Their culture of complaint and studied
Loss, the joylessness of shares declared like
Ledger-lines on squares of bunkered turf.
Their resurrected merger unconfirmed,
Each golf-ball settles like an oracle.

Swimming Coach

Her scoop-neck tee-shirt advertises health,
Her hair in training plaits, her heart the dazzling
Logo of a fish. She trains her class
In tannoy talk, to hear things twice and swim

The water's big indiscipline
That vexes her creation, gift of speech
And lengths of splashless crawl. The pool's
Few luxuries, keep-fit music and the juice bar's

Coloured drinks, cluster at the pane,
Replicate perfection in her tideless baths
As if addicted to the glass.
The pool adjusts, the light turns into fire;

At every stroke the whistle blows in spurts
Of processed air that's hard to breathe.
In drown-quick trunks, her swimmers reach our shore
So after keeps on looking like before.

Polecat

We hunted him with bread, an old
Bin lid and watched his exhibition
With a waterhose; a smile for dragging
Birds to death and nibbling on a scent.

We caught him in the barrow with a plank,
Our open-handed spade and half
A chair-leg sharp for fights.
The birds applaud the snap and shape

Of pain, the roar and belly of his fear.
The flies ascend to scent and start to boil,
His handbag body made the garden spin
And turns him like old china with the soil.

Rear View of a Combine

Walking behind our combine
    in the exhaust and rain of hayseed

I hold my arms our scarecrowing along.
    these fields are blankets on a line

my arms begin, so I wave in the diesel wake
    and watch the wind

to where the thresher's been.
    The smoke from Daniel's compost fire

smarts and burns my eyes. The sound
    of the cutter pins my senses to

to the ground. The line and blankets
    break in layer on layer as high

as I can see.
    Last April maybe Benny's
dad had stinging in his eyes

as he climbed the gorge
    and threw himself away (because of

the drought, Benny said, but others
    say different). And I notice

Noah's rook on the hookboard of the trailer
    as we turn the combine round

latch it up and head for home.

The Bureau for Continuous Mortality

Difficult to take, like Our Lady of Lourdes,
The cave of light and miracle of stones,
The Bureau for Continuous Mortality comes through
In a desk of bills and ads for loans.

Disclosed in blurs, the sun begins
To beckon the authorities keep its pavements
Clean, the Municipal yearbook's different sorts
Of praise, in word of mouth, in payments

Planting paradise. We speak through posters
Like Yahweh after Babel,
The desks laid out by the drinks machine
And deadening click of the door.

Mortality's a fashion mag, an easy masterpiece
At closing time, a special script for rock,
The last man spilling drinks, an empty car,
The camera switched to flashgun for the dark.

Call Centre

Snapshots aren't enough; her hair done crinkle
Style with long-stay eyebrows plucked for hype
And merciful repression in her lips.
With a frieze of stapled notices behind,

Like a drafted book, 'Fax Here Express.'
The chapter on the in-tray waits review.
She shares her floor with Plato Glass,
The billboard's bulging letters and the boss

Whose door reads 'Contracts, Claims and Life'
As if he's everything, and gazes down
To touch her portrait up with facial cream.
As noise comes through the plexiglass

She disapproves and proves all flesh is grass.

Quarry Street

The shops must be in Lent; the butcher's floor
Is up for smells. The grocer's counting fruit
From Panama. The boys from Dresden sulk,
Their china racked by moments of the sun.
A hobbling bee adjusts the scullery plant.
The spinster's dumpy shopping feeds no-one
But herself. Her diary of death-dates weighs
Heavily on her coat. In rooms of coal-
Gas and petunias, where laundry hangs
Its sign accompanying miracles, her pot
Piano sprouts a flash of green. Someone
Probes a bonfire back, restoring fruit forbidden
On the tree, like the words of Panama
That draw the blinds and flick the sign to closed.

Crofting – Llantysilio

Lodged in a part barn
and tethered to croft
is the one who works the raw stone and weather.
His bit back to know
Season by night and hard wood
For its crack in burning.
Wintercome
He'll climb miles round
Corries. Sheep between
The rubble piles
Are taken back to pen.
And then he thinks on thaw
Beside a charring branch.
Lodged in a barn, part of snow,
It's not his voice that calls
The cold, but the dog who will
Perhaps die this year.
The crofter doesn't talk.
It's death other than to nod
To stern things.
In summer
The fence gate will open
Letting his visitor son come home
And the sheep out to graze.

Snowman

The snowman leaves his eyes outside all year.
The coal he saw with, kicked apart, suggests
A mansion-size, an iceberg for the house.
The leaves that fell before him bloomed an inch
Then shuddered like old wisdoms and went slack.

Such massive preparations of the year,
The purple sky for snow, the garden rinsed
And useless, a sense of imperfection
Where the porch begins to bloom: a squall
Of wild December brings him in to blossom twice

With coal. In double deaths of frost and rain
He gleams among his garden to be gone
And practices his monstrous size for June.
His hat and apparatus of his face
And storms he flew through, finish in the sea.

For the first plastered house in Newport

That boat has broken the shed
Where it rattled all winter
And kneels through the wall
With a necklace of tyres. The sea

Is shovelling the top step
Of the beach for the slipway that fell
Apart like a whale's backbone.
Engines are tying knots with smoke

And boathouses dream of water.
The boats are still spilling
The sea and turning home
Like someone working in from sleep.

The sand gathered the first
Plastered house, a nest
Of slats for a tanker and the circular
Saw from a wood yard.

The sound is the sea: an escalator
Four floors and a basement.
The boathouse is on the sun roof,
The building-site of the sea.

Wrecks, Night

Cars have come from water
That forgets them. Winter we pulled
From a pond to see how far
The cold went in, lays a carpet
For the ice and lifts for dogs

Its long interpretation of the cold.
Fuel tanks drift in a whole earth
Of water where trees throw
Down their fire, and the moon
Its bag of rain sideways to surprise.

Saint Jerome at the Court of King Cunedda

The boats come up,
A full mother carrying wood
So Portuguese, brush tapestry,
Castle and ships of Flemish flax.
Cargoes of the fatter kind
Maintain a moat Lord Ferdinand designed
And from his armour's sharpest smile
This gashed expansion through his enemies.

Courtyards of the Jews became
A shelter for the Saint
Whose lion bones, well-traded now
Mosaic a Celtic shrine.
At Asia's lip they make the Saint.
His hat a Brugges lace-maker sent.

The Man in Bull-Bay Lighthouse

The docks are a prison; sound
Captured by the headland. A box
At the harbour wall dredges

Colours untouched since shells
Grew from sea-spit.
A tiny saviour boat

Pulls a coaster's belly
Past the jailer cliffs
And disturbs in the light my house

Grinds: how many surfaces
Move inside the sea.

Sleepy Eye

Locked out and left to tremble in the first
October cold, the drunks rehearse a bus queue
Smashed on Bells and cheap white wine. Their small
Parade to sleep's beneath a billboard's long advertisement,

Commercial Street's short railway arch and sky.
They wake as if a leg's too long and quarrel
Over Racing Pinks and bags with nothing in,
The hoarding's yards of breakfast high above them

Like a dream, its fifteen feet
Of smiles and family bliss. They then explore
Their bedroom like a shelf of knocked-down drinks,
Take care to seem a jumble-sale

Or washing thrown away. So much
Of sleeping Thursday off is shuffling in a heap
Or trying bits of pavement out for size.
Sleep re-designs their Okey-Cokey

Overcoats more like sofas than three men,
And brings them out like building-sites
Dug over for spring; artists by accident
Of Sleepy-Eye which turns the sky to black.

News stand

In costly kit and 'I've been bad' chemise,
The news vendor strikes up his Morning Posts.
With impact culture's stack of strip cartoons,
Not fun but easy: everything's at risk;
The dotcom boom, the price of fuel decode
The century we're in:
The tricky win and little time to live.
And Bargains-of-the-Week, strange death in words.
In workouts with the posters selling drink.
Ordered, fun, stretched out in cries of love,
The news stand selling copies trust-and-take,
Makes way for a work and confidence and light
Prone to swift consensus with the fake.

Pleasure Beach

Noisy lover short of cash, each season
Sells excitement, sex and the best of luck;
More prone to quick consensus with the fake,
Bad alphabets, scraped railings and new paint,

The amusement park is always opening up:
With rescue-bids and hand-me-outs, trying
For impact in the old routines, as if
To come before its time, and afterwards

Were tricks that only seasides can perform.
The sea constructs a line by different rules,
And prone to swift consumption with the new
In simple mediocrity appeal.

With Tequilla slammers, Fonda workouts
The tricky wins with little time to lose.
The roller-coaster rides break every rule
With shrieks of love, the devil let me choose.

Body Shop

Small space, big show, the Body Shop's laid out
Like a love-boutique with Chi-Chi rugs and
Must-have bottles, rows of shape-and-toner,
The Dr Action Diet Revolution.

A swish of a floral hem and crepe de chine,
Face-pack tightening for hours, the mind restored,
The tissue box for wiping off the gel,
From a bed of peppermint and sizal salt.

Our guide to free expression of the soul,
Purchase what you can't possess, like Paris,
Meaning and moments held in the future.
In the shop's recorded struggle with space

The perfume shelves display new fragrances;
The therapy bags, margins of expression
That crazy charm for laughter-lines that show
The face turns into ice to cure the heart.

Softball game in the Lifers' yard

Expert with calendars, with fake IDs
The man who runs the lifers' softball team,
With shocking story-twist and constant shake,
Converts the garden to our softball park.

Our game's a sound of names and sets of grief,
Interpretations of adversity
In lives beyond the fence, the old outside.
The edgy boxer's new protection game

Who keeps the score and knows what we are worth.
As when our fielders, flatfoot, square and deep
Experience time in different ways:
The mechanics of escape, the future long

In curled-up photographs and curly hair,
Like Pharaoh's bouncer understanding dreams.
Our team of six strings out along the square,
Mundane and tensionless and mystery-free

Like Sunday morning's faith-revival-hour.
Our catcher standing free across the park
Confesses softball makes us hard to see:
His slow retreat from history made alone,

A break-up call from Molly on the phone.

Faith Healer

In best-behaviour clothes, black mission shoes
Interpreting the world as illnesses,
With restless bright blue eyes and curly hair,
Our healer's ways are small, deliberate,

He shares the afternoon with broken lives,
Those from detox, some from Self-Awareness,
Some from Mind Replacement Therapy,
Some with everything to cure: finding home,

Their marriage, psycho-sex and Back Pain Week.
Prepared in balanced sentences, his gift
Abandons pain and then expresses it.
To take each moment further separately,

Small illnesses, a laying on of hands.
Bought and turned to trash then brought again,
The global hunting for the next big thing,
Arrives in kit and I've been bad chemise.

Painters

It must make a great difference, setting your
Ladder in the crocuses, taking weight
On the rung with a portable radio
And the awkward pressure of the brushes,

Learning to see split-level bungalows
In the Dulux Colour Scheme. Appearing
Against the glass, the beaten-up furniture,
Computers, old dogs and owners

With a finger in the brochure for Spring.
Stepping back, allowing the gloss to dry
And picking up the cast-off cans for home,
Overalls splashed and the day turning dark

The engine ticking over to depart.

Pearl

The sun grinds a ring in the sea;
Cliffs generate sand through

The gills of a fish and
Irritate the dark.

Saint Cecelia's catacomb.
The sky is that feature of the sea

For which
Claudius waves his white hard head.

Branwell

Your sisters were the fury: games pulsed
Like Luddites through the house.
Yorkshire grew its gem inside your eye
And matured the moon's pearl.
But they took you for a signalman
And the broken teeth of Latin
Made a crime of introspection.
They ground out Haworth
Like grit in a shell
And women turned the amber
Of your eye to chalk.
In the spin of liquor
He looked from your forehead
A blank, sacked clerk.
The sky grew its cataract
Clouds against the eyes.
You could not know
Your sister did not eat
Which later killed her child.

View of the Ballcrane Driver

The cab opens its head to the snow and a Freightliner
Dodge holds its backbone. How the huge
Affect so little high in the process
Of the junk-yard. The stroke of the two-band
Chainsaw breaks a whisper
From the wrecks and moves over the stacked saloons

Like a '98 Buick. The ballcrane rattles through
A double roofed Ford softer than glass,
Adjusting the lights over forty feet.
The attractive opens; the ballcrane
Breaks a ten-ton universal called 'Alice'.
The sixteen levers thrash

And a gearbox somersaults
To the corner. Through the sides of cars
I return into view, silver as a headlamp
And covered with the winter of a lightweight
Chassis till the snow pulls all its clothes away
And the crane rubs out its circle from the yard.

Salvaging the Picturedrome

The wood stirs; high
In the unsalvaged rafterbeams
That hold their bolts too well
My brother is hammering the dark
For iron. I can hear his mouth
Pull the breath from the air. We will use
The wood no more he lifts down
Time after time full of rain.
I find a seat I cannot take
For the damp and with a salvage lamp
That drips search the scrap
He takes to open the head
Of the Picturedrone, his light
Far inside the screen, the past
On the other side of air
Brighter than the bathhouse with its brass.

Fishing for Horses

The haystacks bulge like the bellies of two men.
The stream shakes down its stones into Jenkins' pool
Where the carp are in the eye of the chicken.
August, clean and empty as the bones of a dog
Strides over Pont-y-ffridd, and we sling for fish
Into this thinnest part of Wales.
The rabbit waits to catch the fox, the seed
Desires the sparrow. The air chases horses
Out of Gwynnedd that slow and let us watch.
We reply, reel in our lines and let them pass.

Pentre

Over Jenkins' pool the day moves backwards.
The farm squats fertile as a pig
And the hill is in the water. The air
Hammering at the aslant fields
Rolls its thumbprint over Jenkins' pool.
The day is round as the head of a sparrow.

My hand closes like the ribs
Of a dog. I look inside to find the map.
The pages bend to catch the dark.
Picked out in the light of a farmhouse
I notice the drunk from town
Swinging late and early home across the border.

Cnicht, Spring

The tree holds up its hair
And takes its jewels down.
The snow for April turns to green
And a barn
Strips at the edge of town,
Collapses into its own darkness
And disappears.

The grass stands out to see
A tree fall backwards into the lake
And resists my fingers
Holding up its arms
A crowd for holy Easter.

Afternoon in a Deserted Scrapyard

The past stopped at eighty-thousand .
I kneel on the engine, stripping it down
With a spanner at the back. The yard is

Heavy with years falling in. I breathe
On the glass and disappear inside this
Strongbox as I pull the profit out of

A sixties Ford: the carburettor
Lifts out into mid-air where a blinding
Capri is nosing from this world, its mouth

Broken a week ago. My head lightens
At the root of the yard beneath a roof
Of shanties in joint too long.

Something covered in '95 oil
Is working its escape, to stay and keep
The grace that travelling forward gives away.

View from Building Twenty

A gust across the rain pool shakes the sky.
Our radio tunes lost ships, odd morse, a voice
Past Asia on the dial as aircraft drone
Into airport lights and storms collect the night,
The stars obey the water where they lie.

The radio loses everything: an early news,
An untuned sunset, language we can't place,
Music trembling in the shipping news
That dies and reconstructs, like Jehova's
Favourite animal, the bee, in early

Re-arrangement of the day, comes of age
Returning to its roots, and midnight moths
Still flickering at the dawn, perform
A voice confirming this is Paradise,
As earth swerves out of darkness into storm.